A John Catt Publication

The first in a new series

C000301522

Everyone Succeeds

Steve Margetts

Foreword by
Andy Buck

Leadership Matters in action

"A compelling insight into how to run a school that puts improving teaching at the heart of what it does"
Doug Lemov

LEADERSHIP MATTERS
With You, For You

First published 2018
by John Catt Educational Ltd,
12 Deben Mill Business Centre, Old Maltings Approach,
Melton, Woodbridge IP12 1BL

Tel: +44 (0) 1394 389850 Fax: +44 (0) 1394 386893
Email: enquiries@johncatt.com
Website: www.johncatt.com

ISBN: 978 1 911 382 69 0

Set and designed by John Catt Educational Limited

Contents

To the fantastic staff, students, and governors of Torquay Academy.
This is what we do.

Foreword

When I wrote *Leadership Matters*, I had no idea how it would catch on. Unbelievably, it is now one of the best-selling school leadership books on Amazon! But while the book does include numerous examples gathered from successful schools, it never sought to tell the story of a particular school's journey. In this sense, it is incomplete. How do we know that the combination of ideas presented will work if implemented?

Which is why I am just so excited that Steve Margetts has written this book. In describing how Torquay Academy has become one of the fastest-improving schools in the country, *Everyone Succeeds* is an authentic and inspiring account of how great leadership at all levels in a school really does matter. In this *tour-de-force*, Steve has brought to life many of the principles that underpin the original *Leadership Matters* book.

In his characteristically self-deprecating way, he sets out a compelling narrative for school improvement in which he generously shares the secrets of Torquay Academy's success. Seriously rooted in the work of the likes of Doug Lemov, Paul Bambrick-Santoyo and Simon Sinek, this book is a thoughtful and reflective account of how he and his team have taken these seminal influences and translated them into sustained and embedded practice in their school.

Crucially, however, the senior team's approach has been to take these powerful ideas and then intelligently adapt them to suit their context. To paraphrase Dylan Wiliam: *everything will work somewhere; nothing works everywhere; the critical question is, what will work here?* In offering up their own journey, the school is not suggesting it has the definitive blueprint for school improvement. Instead, it has sought to share what has worked for them. It leaves the reader to do exactly what they did – intelligently filter the possibilities and then apply them with rigour and care.

Steve's approach has also not been about quick fixes. It has been rooted in building a sustainable future for the school, echoing many of the sentiments expressed in the concept of *architect leadership* espoused by Dr Ben Laker and the team at the Centre for High Performance. Leaders at all levels have focused on creating a truly impressive culture and climate, concepts at the heart of *Leadership Matters*.

In this context, culture is taken to mean *the way we do things around here* and relates to the systems, procedures and standard practices and, in particular, to the high standards and expectations that exist in the way these are delivered. A useful way of thinking of culture is to consider what someone new joining a school would see happening on a day-to-day basis and the extent to which everyone is working in the same way. Is there a consistent set of high expectations about how staff plan and deliver great lessons? Are the learning environments inspiring and well organised? Do pupils have strong and supportive relationships with their peers and all the staff they work with? Do all classrooms offer, as Mary Myatt so eloquently puts it in her book of the same title, high challenge and low threat? Is there an assumption that everyone succeeds? All these are central to Torquay Academy's success.

Of course, it's easy to think that creating a great culture is all that matters. But it is only half of this school's story. It has also worked hard to create an impressive climate, which is more about how it *feels* to work in the school. This reflects the morale, how appreciated staff feel and the degree of trust within the staff as a whole. This is much more difficult to describe or measure, but research in the wider business arena has shown that the effect of climate on team productivity is considerable.

Taken together, the more positive the culture and climate one creates, the more likely staff are to go the extra mile. This concept is known as *discretionary effort*. It is described as the input from individuals over and above what they must contribute to keep their jobs. In Torquay Academy, the sense of discretionary effort is palpable from the moment you walk through the door. And it's not about staff working longer hours. It is much more about an attitude where all colleagues, teachers, and support staff, want to be a bit better today than they were yesterday. The school that has resulted is quite remarkable.

I hope you enjoy reading about their amazing journey as much as I have!

Andy Buck

Managing Director

Leadership Matters

Introduction

'Everything works somewhere,
nothing works everywhere.'
Dylan William

We believe an excellent school is built upon seven pillars. Effective leadership and implementation of each of these pillars can lead to an excellent school where everyone succeeds. They are:

- Why, vision and culture
- Student behaviour
- Teaching and learning
- We can all get better
- Curriculum
- Data analysis and self-evaluation
- Leadership at all levels

Neglecting one of these areas will have a negative impact on the school and its students. The following table demonstrates the result of underperformance of one of the pillars – for example, poor 'leadership at all levels' will lead to 'no direction and drive' in the school.

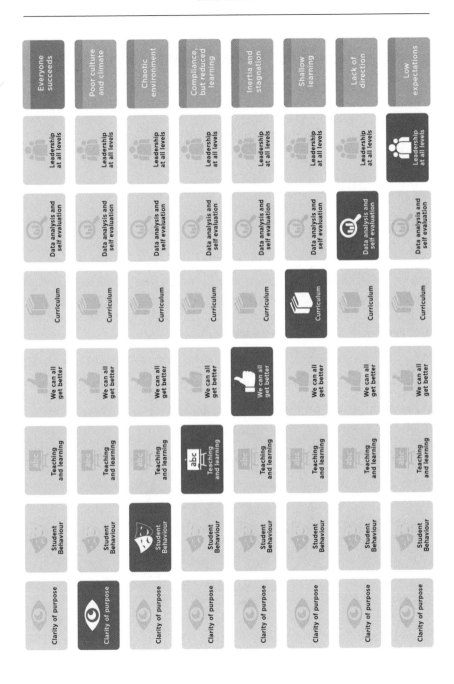

Clarity of purpose

'What will and won't work is a
question of timing and culture.'
Kieran Earley

Start with why

The first time I heard Sir David Carter talk, he spoke of the importance of knowing why your school existed. He recommended reading Simon Sinek's book *Start With Why*, within which the latter argues that businesses should answer why they exist before they decide what they do and how they do it. To help explain this concept, he developed the 'Golden Circle', which has three layers:

Why – This is the core belief of the business. It's why the business exists.

How – This is how the business fulfils that core belief.

What – This is what the company does to fulfil that core belief.

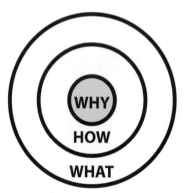

While this sounds simple, Sinek found that most companies answer these questions in the wrong order. They start with 'what' they do and then move to 'how' they do it; the vast majority neglect to mention *'why'* they do what they do.

Why was an easy question for me to answer as it coincided with my own desire to lead a school in Torquay Academy's situation. It was important for the senior team and governors to have statements that we could agree upon and use to support future decisions. The 'whys' that lie at the heart of our golden circle are:

- Everyone succeeds.
- Students first.
- We believe that every student who joins TA has the ability to go on to university.

These statements underpin all that we do; when we discuss an issue, we ask ourselves: does this support our 'why'? Difficult decisions are made easier when you know they will strengthen the 'whys' that underpin our school's existence.

The words 'everyone succeeds' are prominent in the school – you see them everywhere: etched into the glass, printed on the walls, on the front of every exercise book. These aren't just words, they stand for everything we do.

Once we were clear about our 'why', the 'how' and 'what' were simple to add:

How

- A culture of the highest expectations.
- Inspirational teachers who enthuse a love of learning.
- A wealth of academic, sporting, creative arts, and vocational opportunities.
- The best care for all of our children.
- Every lesson is aspirational, challenging, and thought-provoking.

What

- Students become the best they can be and get the grades that enable them to move onto their next steps in life.

- They are principled, resilient and will be valued members of society.
- TA is the first-choice school for students and parents in Torquay.

KEY POINT

Be clear about your why. Share it with staff, governors, students, and parents. Make it visible and keep sharing it.

A clear vision

After joining Torquay Academy in January 2014, I wanted to create a vision that was owned by the whole school and its community. We used part of our first day back, which was an INSET, to ask our staff to visualise the school we aspired to have as a beacon in the heart of our community. Everyone contributed under 12 headings that I felt reflected the key areas of the school:

1. Teaching and learning

2. Celebrating success, behaviour and attendance

3. Pastoral support and personal development

4. Community and parents

5. Pedagogy and curriculum

6. Beyond the curriculum

7. Narrowing the gaps

8. Data and reporting (especially relating to students' performance)

9. Culture

10. Leadership (senior; governance; middle; classroom; student)

11. Finance and IT platform

12. Strategy

To ensure the vision document was fully representative of everyone who has an interest in the success of the school, we invited other stakeholders' views as well. These thoughts were then assembled and drafted into Version 1 of our vision. Staff groups re-assembled to finalise our vision over several meetings.

The completed version was 16 pages of quite detailed text. We shared it with students, parents, staff, and the local community, but I wanted a more digestible Vision 2020. I contacted the brilliant Joel Cooper, an artist who I had met at an SSAT conference, in the hope he could bring our vision to life. He produced this graphic of the key points:

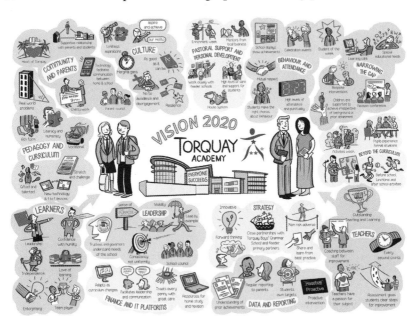

Joel then made some adjustments, so it would fit onto an 8m by 2m wall in the heart of the school. We are delighted with the results; I will often talk to students during the day in front of the wall and discuss various aspects of our vision. It is also a talking point for all of our visitors, including our National Schools Commissioner, Sir David Carter.

The vision is the platform for the changes that we implemented during the first year. Tasks were aligned with the 12 areas of the vision; we all knew what we were trying to achieve.

KEY POINT

A vision about the school you want to become is only powerful if it is shared with the whole community.

Culture and climate

There was a culture that we wanted to establish in the school community; this would impact upon both staff and students. Our 'why' is the foundation of the climate and culture we wanted to create.

The culture had to change to one that is underpinned by having the highest expectations of every member of the community where success would be the norm. This meant ensuring it was OK to be the student who wanted to listen, work, and excel – that student becomes the norm rather than the exception. This required a significant shift in the mindset of a significant number of our community of students, staff, and parents. This was no longer going to be the sink school in a small coastal local authority dominated by grammar schools.

There is a continuous message of the importance of learning and knowledge. There were far too many disruptions to lessons with various trips and visits: the mantra 'teachers in front of students' was therefore repeated again and again. We made decisions to support this. No trips would be allowed during term time, and a new threshold for CPD was introduced (this will be discussed in more detail later).

KEY POINT

It is vital that all of our students have five brilliant lessons every day of the school year. Beyond ensuring their safety and happiness, there is nothing more important.

Honours boards have been placed at the entrance to the school where we celebrate some of the most important aspects of the school: students who have gone to university, 100% attendance, outstanding effort, sports and performing arts colours and Head Boy and Head Girl. We celebrate stars in each subject every half term and certificates are awarded for accumulating house points. Students are proud to wear badges awarded for these, and many other, achievements.

Building a sense of community was also important for me. We meet as a whole school in the Sports Hall for an assembly at the end of every half term, and a weekly blog is published on our website. Both of these are opportunities to celebrate success – we want the school to be a place where students are proud of their achievements.

Assemblies

Whole-school assemblies are an opportunity for me to relay key messages to the school community, repeat them and follow them up with school displays and initiatives. The following are key themes that are revisited on a regular basis:

- Thankfulness
- Climbing the mountain to university
- Every student can go on to university
- Austin's butterfly
- Moving along the bell curve to achieve higher grades
- Hard work

Pygmalion cycle

The Pygmalion cycle demonstrates the phenomenon whereby higher expectations lead to an increase in performance. It is based upon *Pygmalion in the Classroom*, a 1968 book by Robert Rosenthal and Lenore Jacobson. It relates to our culture and climate of ensuring everyone feels they can achieve more than they imagined possible and then setting it in motion. It required a shift from the previous expectations of teachers, parents, and students – everyone needed to raise their expectations, and this had to start with the teachers. There is no place here for adults who couldn't shift their expectations from a low-performing secondary modern to one where every child progresses and succeeds.

We set highly ambitious target grades for every student, and they are non-negotiable.

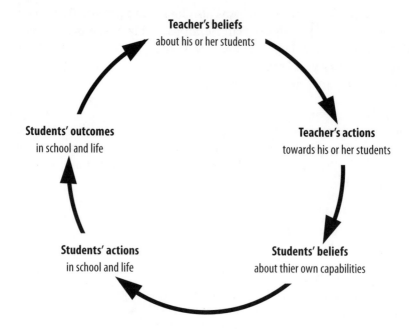

The highest expectations

We have the highest expectations of every member of the school community in every situation. We do not believe that past performance, background or indeed any other factor should have a negative impact on achievement and progress. We don't look out of our window looking for excuses to explain our students' achievement and progress; white working class, coastal town, high unemployment, low aspirations, high pupil premium, grammar school authority – you won't ever hear us using these as reasons to explain away outcomes. The outcomes are our responsibility, and we have the power to affect them.

Marginal gains

We equated our approach to that of Dave Brailsford and how he transformed British Cycling into world-beaters. We would use the principles of marginal gains to make small improvements to every area of the school; the result of this, we hoped, would be a transformational change.

Each aspect of the school was identified and discussed to identify improvements. Leaders then had responsibility for implementing the changes. All staff are able, and positively encouraged, to email their suggestions for marginal gains. There is no belief that all of the answers lie within the SLT.

Every second counts

This is a key message that runs throughout the school. We remind ourselves of the impact of losing just a small amount of time every lesson:

- 3 minutes lost per lesson
- 5 lessons a day
- 15 minutes lost each day
- 190 days a year
- 79 hours lost per year
- 9.5 days lost per year
- Over a third of a school year during their time at TA

We continually search for ways to reduce the wasting of time.

KEY POINT

Every second a student is in school is precious. You can't afford to waste a moment.

Controllables and uncontrollables

We are very aware of those things within our control and those beyond it. Controllables and uncontrollables are identified in all areas of the school, and we ensure that we control the controllables! With the changes to the examination systems, there are fewer controllables in that area, but there are still plenty of others: attendance, quality of teaching, homework completion, exam prep *etc.* Don't leave anything to chance if it's within your control.

Non-negotiables

It is important to us that we are clear about what our non-negotiables are. These are the aspects of the school that are centrally set and must be followed by all. Staff and students are clear about our non-negotiables and what the consequences are if they aren't followed. Unless you provide clarity over your non-negotiables, you have no right to be disappointed or upset when they aren't adhered to.

Consistency

Consistency, not uniformity, is our goal in all areas of the school. This is a thread that runs thick throughout. Andy Buck's Giraffe Concept describes how all giraffes have long necks, but it is the markings that vary between different animals; 'long-neck issues' are those where consistency is required, and 'markings issues' are those where variability is acceptable. We have more long-neck issues than markings ones.

Procedures, systems and routines

The sublime relies on the mundane. With our focus upon the controllables, non-negotiables and consistency, we have to plan our systems and procedures to the finest detail. We believe our students and staff benefit from this.

Doug Lemov, author of *Teach Like a Champion*, identifies the relationship between systems, procedures and routines as:

- Procedure: explicit guidance on how to execute a recurring task – *eg*, working independently; answering questions in class
- System: a network of related procedures that help teachers accomplish end goals – *eg*, managing behaviour, moving materials, participating in a discussion
- Routine: a procedure or system that students execute automatically and without teacher prompting

One way of helping to embed these routines is the partnership work with the primary schools. Tom Thatcher (Assistant Principal, Maths and Cross-Phase) oversees a joint leadership working party with our largest feeder school. This, combined with the work of Dan Jones (Academic Progress Leader for Year 7 and Head of Transitions), ensures that students who join us already have an understanding of our routines.

CATSx reviews

We undertake CATSx reviews throughout the year. CATSx is the continuous quality assurance of each process within a system. Each process in the school is identified and labelled either:

- Confirm – It is working well and we should continue with it in its current form.
- Adjust – We like the process, but it needs to be tweaked in order for it to be more effective.
- Transform – The objective of the process is still a target, but we need to reassess how we try and achieve it.
- Scrap – It's a waste of everyone's time.

The 'x' refers to the constant desire to seek and establish new routines that will improve the school:

- eXtra – Seek out new processes to improve current practice.

The review is underpinned by the principle of marginal gains.

Key action points

- ☐ Identify your why.
- ☐ Decide how you will share your 'why', 'how' and 'what' with your community.
- ☐ Create a vision: have a clear idea of what kind of school you want to become.
- ☐ What is the culture and climate you are trying to achieve? What are the key areas that require change?
- ☐ What are the key areas of student success that you wish to acknowledge? How do you celebrate that success?
- ☐ Do your target grades underpin the Pygmalion cycle? If not, change them.
- ☐ Dissect your school, look for the marginal gains in each area and then implement them.
- ☐ What are your non-negotiables? Agree on them and share them with the school.
- ☐ What are your long-neck and markings issues?

Ideas you can implement in your school

☐ A local signwriter will be able to put your key messages around the school. Text looks great when it is black vinyl on white walls; or grey vinyl on glass gives an effective etched glass look.

☐ Use every opportunity you can to reinforce your vision's key messages.

☐ The price of badges and other rewards has fallen recently as many new suppliers have entered the market. Can you review your rewards systems to better celebrate success and effort?

Student behaviour

'The standard you walk past is
the standard you accept.'
Lieutenant General David Morrison

Without dramatic improvements in the behaviour of our students, there could be no value in making any other changes to the school. Far too many students arrived when it suited them, opted out of lessons too often, disrupted the learning of others in class and told staff what they thought of them when challenged.

Uniform

If you aren't in the correct uniform, you don't go to lessons or have morning and lunch breaks. If a student arrives with incorrect uniform, there is a consequence, but we try to fix the problem. Spare uniforms are kept and lent to students to enable them to go to lessons; if uniform problems can't be fixed, then the student is kept in isolation. Parents are informed if a student doesn't have the correct uniform. There is one senior leader, Ben Chadwick (Assistant Principal – Student behaviour), who has the final say on all issues regarding uniform. This ensures consistency throughout the school.

Punctuality and a calm start

Punctuality was a significant issue in the school. Students arrived around the 8.30am bell (the official start time); some days it felt like as many arrived after the bell as before it. One day I counted over 100 students (out of a school of 800 back in 2014) arriving through the gate after 8.30am; of course, they were even later by the time they reached their classrooms.

We had a complete overhaul of the start of the day and our expectations about punctuality. We say, 'Being on time is getting there ten minutes early'. We decided to open the canteen at 7.30am, and we offer a free healthy breakfast to all staff and students. Many take up this offer, and the school is a busy place from very early on.

At 8.20am a bell indicates that it is time for all staff and students to go outside. Each year group has their own area where they line up in their tutor groups in alphabetical order. They line up in silence. During this time tutors can be seen looking for uniform issues, year leaders pass on messages and SLT hand out detention cards.

Another bell at 8.27am leads to two things. Firstly, the student entrance gate is shut. Any student arriving after this time goes to a late group with a Vice Principal and they receive lunchtime detention. There is a giant digital clock on the front of the school to provide transparency. You will see children running down the road and up the drive to ensure they aren't late. Secondly, students file into tutor groups in single file and silence. By 8.30am all students (apart from, on average, two to six who are late out of a school of 1350) are sat in silence in their tutor rooms ready for a day of learning.

We believe our calm start to the day leads to a calmer day.

Equipment check

At the start of each tutor session, there is an equipment check. Students are expected to have the following equipment in a 30cm clear pencil case:

- 3 black pens
- 2 purple pens
- 3 pencils
- Pencil sharpener
- Rubber
- Clear 12" ruler
- Highlighter
- Protractor

- Metal safety compass
- Compass pencil
- Casio FX83 GTPLUS scientific calculator
- Glue stick

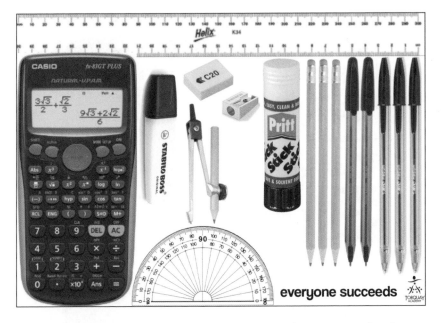

If a student doesn't have the correct equipment, they receive a lunchtime detention.

Transitions

We want to minimise the time between finishing learning in one classroom and starting again in another. To support this, all year, leaders and free SLT are in the main atrium during transitions to ensure students move quickly and via the most direct route. They walk with their pencil cases out to save time packing it away and getting it out again. When students enter or leave the learning areas (department corridors off the main atrium), they do so in silence. Students are greeted by their teachers (who are standing at the classroom doors), enter the room and start their Do Now task in silence.

Lesson behaviour management

Many schools will be familiar with the three-tier approach we take in lessons. After the third warning, a student is parked in the behaviour centre for the remainder of that lesson. Parents are contacted, and students receive a 60-minute detention on the same evening (this is extended to 90 minutes if they misbehave or don't work effectively). The teacher who parked the student will visit them during the detention to reinforce expectations in the classroom, build bridges to ensure learning can effectively take place in the following lesson and deliver any positive messages.

KEY POINT

Grudges can't be held from lesson to lesson. Learning is too important. However hard it can be on particular occasions, we have to remember that we are the adults and professionals.

We are clear about how we expect to see students sitting in lessons; posters remind them of this. We would challenge a student who is slouched or not sat facing forwards with their legs under the table.

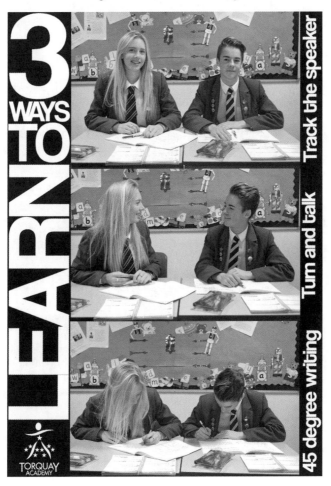

SLANT is an acronym used at Torquay Academy to remind students of how we want them to sit:

- Sit up straight
- Listen
- Answer questions
- Never interrupt
- Track the teacher

Exercise books

We have bespoke exercise books produced for every subject, and they are kept in a plastic wallet. On the back cover, there are the names of the three top universities where that subject can be studied, three jobs that subject can lead to and three reasons to study the subject. Keywords are on the inside back cover, and subjects choose what is most relevant for them for the inside front cover.

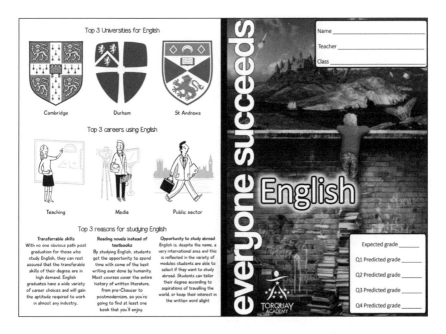

The poster on the following page outlines how we expect students to write in their books. It is also the background on all school computers to serve as a constant reminder.

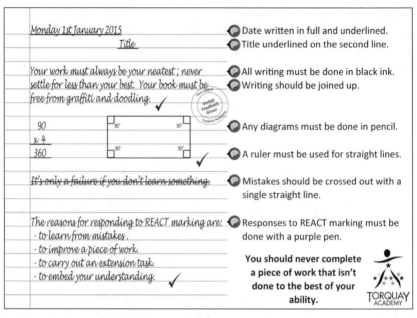

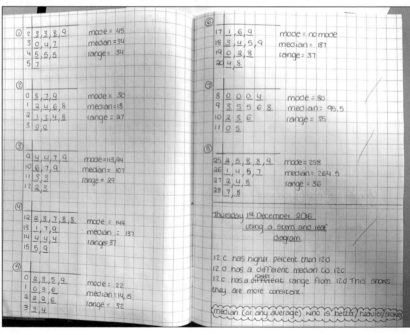

Eliminate defiance and reasonable requests

One problem we often faced was students refusing to do what a member of staff asked them to do. Refusing to leave a room when parked, not going to detention when asked, or running away when instructed to go to our behaviour centre; all of these were often accompanied with verbal abuse. We do not accept students refusing to follow a reasonable request or verbally abusing staff. Fixed term exclusions are used whenever this occurs.

Clear boundaries

There are rules, and there are consequences. If you are late, don't have the correct equipment or full uniform, fail to complete homework, swear, chew gum or get parked from a lesson, you will have a detention. It's black and white. Our students are aware of this, and there can be no argument about the sanction as it is totally transparent.

All transgressions are consistently applied; you should not have favourites who escape sanctions or others who face extra ones because they are deemed to be troublemakers.

KEY POINT

Whatever path you choose to follow, you must ensure that every infraction is followed up every time. It should always be easier for the student to do the right thing. This means that students who do meet expectations don't see others getting away with it.

Centrally run detentions

All of our detentions are managed by Assistant Principal Ben Chadwick and run centrally by SLT. Teachers are not expected to run detentions or chase up students who miss them. This enables them to focus on teaching, planning, and marking. The central point and single member of staff overseeing the systems also ensure that no student gets away with missing a consequence.

Safeguarding and pastoral care

The safety and wellbeing of our students is a central thread of the school.

We have the highest expectations of our students, but we also care deeply. Our safeguarding team is led by our Designated Safeguarding Lead, Elaine Watling.

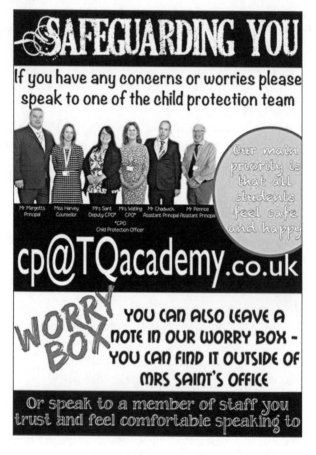

Each year group has a teacher who oversees academic progress and a full-time pastoral leader who is a member of our support staff.

The TA way: learn like a champion

When Year 7 students join TA, they spend three days learning the TA Way. They follow a bespoke number of lessons, assemblies, and activities to ensure they fully understand what will be expected of them over the next seven years. The sessions are based on the following themes:

- Respect
- Extracurricular life
- Revision, homework, and knowledge organisers
- Reading
- Lesson expectations
- Rules and consequences
- Grit and resilience
- Learn like a champion
- Line up and tutor time

If students join the school during the year, they will receive a cut down version of the TA Way. It is essential every member of our school community is clear about our expectations and how to do things the way we want them done. By being explicit about our systems and procedures and giving students time to practise them, we hope they will become routines.

Key action points

☐ Who has the final say about uniform issues? You can't send out mixed messages from different colleagues.

☐ Does your start of the day set the tone for the rest of the day?

☐ Do your teachers face delays in their lessons because students don't have the correct equipment for their lessons?

☐ Are all students and staff aware of the school's expectations and what will happen if they aren't met?

☐ Do students ever get away with a punishment because they don't turn up?

☐ How do you ensure that all new members of the school community are fully aware of the school's expectations?

Ideas you can implement in your school

☐ Visual reminders of classroom expectations are a useful prompt for staff and students alike.

☐ A stock of spare uniform can help you overcome issues. Leavers can be a good source of this.

☐ Have you told all of your students your expectations of them? Do they understand what you want them to do? If the answer is no, find a way to tell them and keep repeating it!

☐ Ensure no leaders (and ideally no staff) ever walk past something you are unhappy with. Colleagues can't unsee something; they have to deal with it.

Teaching and learning

'The variability between schools in most Western countries is far smaller than the variability within schools, or, more simply, that it matters more which classroom you go to than which school.'
John Hattie

Teach like a champion (TLAC)

I have been a fan of Doug Lemov's *Teach Like a Champion* book for many years as I believe it gives a simplicity and common language to our profession. He describes the book as being 'about the tools of the teaching craft' and describes students who are facing 'a rapidly closing window of opportunity'. I felt that the techniques would enable us to establish a shared language and greater consistency within the school.

We have introduced a TLAC focus every two weeks. All teachers focus on developing one technique, and this is shared with our students. They are shown a PowerPoint by their tutors that explains the technique to them and what they need to do to play their part in the teaching techniques. We ask our students to Learn Like a Champion. Posters around the school are a continuous reminder of this technique. We believe this helps to ensure that the systems and routines established at the start of the year are maintained to the highest standard. If we see the quality of one of the techniques being used starting to slip, it becomes the next TLAC focus.

To help prompt students that teachers are using a particular TLAC technique, we had some icons designed for the key strategies we use; for example, the icons on the next page indicate 'turn and talk' and 'wait time'.

We have also thought carefully about the design of the classrooms and how that can support TLAC techniques. A lectern has been installed in every classroom; it is placed in the corner (in TLAC terminology, the 'Pastore's Perch') to enable the teacher to have the best view of their classroom and 'build their radar'. On the lectern are the teacher's laptop and a visualiser to support 'Show Call'. It was an expensive development, but these marginal gains will improve teaching further.

The 5Rs – our T&L non-negotiables

There are several non-negotiables that we expect to see in each of our lessons. We believe these help to ensure a high floor but no ceiling in the quality of teaching in our classrooms. They also ensure that our students get consistency, which helps to develop their habits and saves time in the classroom. Our non-negotiables are split into five areas, our 5Rs:

Routines

- Threshold – meet and greet at the door.
- Start of the lesson – students to write in their book the title and date (underlined) and then to start working on the 'Do Now' activity on the board.
- SLANT and other TLAC strategies to be used
- Homework must be appropriate and challenging – Knowledge Organiser to be checked by tutor and exam questions by teacher
- End of the lesson – students standing behind a tucked-in chair with their blazer on, silently waiting to be dismissed by the teacher

Relationships

- Praise points: Behaviour points ratio of 5:1
- Consistent use of the Behaviour for Learning policy
- Establish and maintain routines
- Always celebrate success – no matter how small
- Positive rather than negative statements
- Growth Mindset

Resources

- A solid scheme of learning and five-minute learning plan if part of a learning walk or official observation
- Appropriate challenge.

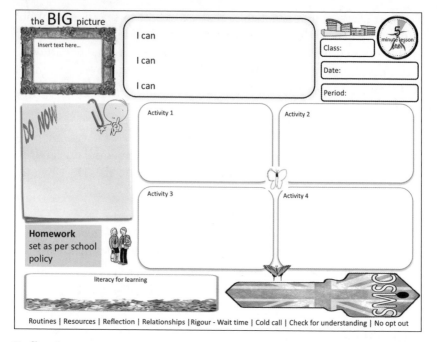

Reflection

- Feedback/Marking (Yellow Stickers) – appropriate, challenging, facilitates student improvement and frequency – staff to use green pens
- Student time to reflect on teacher feedback (build into lessons) – students to use purple pens
- Green Stickers at the front of books (each cycle) to support reflection.

Rigour

- Use of both numeracy and literacy strategies within lessons.
- Use of *Teach Like a Champion* strategies within lessons.
- Pace and Challenge and work the clock.

KEY POINT

A high floor, with no ceiling, is the goal of our non-negotiables.

The 5Rs describe what we would expect to see over time in a teacher's lesson; the following summarises our basic expectations of every lesson:

- Threshold. Staff stand in the doorway of their classroom to welcome the students and ensure that silence is maintained as they start their learning.
- Date and title. It is written in their exercise book and underlined.
- Do Now. Every lesson begins with a silent Do Now. This is an activity that is on the board that students start in silence when they arrive in the classroom. This may be a starter, or a low-stakes knowledge test based on their homework.
- Dismissal. Students stand in silence behind their chairs at the end of the lesson. Uniform is checked, and they must have their pencil case in their hand if they are heading off to another lesson. The teacher will then stand in the doorway as the class is dismissed.

We want consistency throughout the school, so students know exactly what is expected of them and how they should respond in every classroom.

KEY POINT

Consistency, not uniformity, is our goal.

Teaching and learning handbook

We produce our own Teaching and Learning handbook that outlines our way of doing things for every member of staff; TLAC is a thread running throughout it. It acts as a reference guide or manual for teachers to refer to.

It is very different from our staff handbook as it only relates to the expectations of teachers in the classroom. It has proved to be particularly useful for new staff joining the school. They are given a copy on their induction day, enabling them to get a better understanding of the school before joining.

Teaching and learning packs

All of our teachers have a Teaching and Learning pack (T&L pack) for each of their classes. This provides them with the key information they need for that class. While providing the class teacher with invaluable information about their group, it also enables any visitors to the class to contextualise the teaching. Every T&L pack contains the following information, most of which is produced centrally:

- Whole-class data. This is based on prior data and compares the class to both school and national averages.

- Seating plan. The seating plan is determined by the teacher based on their knowledge of their class. The seating plan in the pack includes basic information next to the photograph of every student. It is created using our behaviour management software package.

- Achievement and progress data. Students' data from previous cycles is included. It highlights students who are currently below their expected progress levels. It also shows the difference in progress and achievement between different groups in the class.

- Disadvantaged pupils rationale. It lists the class's financially disadvantaged students along with a range of approaches that can be employed to support them.

- Most able rationale. It lists the class's most able students along with a range of approaches that can be employed to support them.

- SEN one-page profiles. Our excellent SEN team, led by Assistant Principal Glyn Penrice, produce a one-page profile for each SEN student. This provides information, written in collaboration with the student, about their needs and how they can best be met.

- SEN support sheets. These provide additional information about the needs of the students in that class.

Key action points

- ☐ Do you have shared language for teaching techniques?
- ☐ Are your staff clear about your expectations in the classroom? Be clear about your non-negotiables.
- ☐ Do your teachers know the makeup of their classes? If not, the T&L packs may be your answer.

Ideas you can implement in your school

- ☐ Draw up a list of your own non-negotiables. Share them.
- ☐ If you present classroom-based ideas in CPD and you expect staff to implement them straight away in their lessons, you could consider giving them time to practise.
- ☐ If there are teaching techniques, you use in your school find the time to share them with your students.
- ☐ Ensure your teachers know who their disadvantaged and most able pupils are.

We can all get better

'Every teacher needs to improve, not because they are not good enough, but because they can be even better.'
Prof. Dylan Wiliam

The right people on the bus

The acid test for anybody joining the teaching staff at TA is: would I be happy with my own children being taught by them (both of my children are currently at a primary school in our catchment area)? First, we are all teachers and, irrespective of the post being applied for, everyone must be a very good classroom practitioner before we consider a job application. We subscribe to Jim Collins's belief (*from Good to Great*) that the right people are the most important asset in an organisation, rather than simply people in general. We would rather not appoint and find an alternative solution than appoint somebody that we didn't have complete faith in.

> **KEY POINT**
>
> The right teachers are the most important asset to your school, rather than simply teachers in general.

Coaching of teachers

When I was able to visit the Uncommon Schools in New York and New Jersey, in addition to seeing the impact of wonderful teaching on students, I saw the impact of leverage coaching; another area I had long been interested in. We know that our greatest responsibility as senior leaders is to develop and grow our teachers. This is a fact supported by Viviane Robinson's research, as summarised across the page.

44

Robinson - Effects of Leadership on Student Outcomes

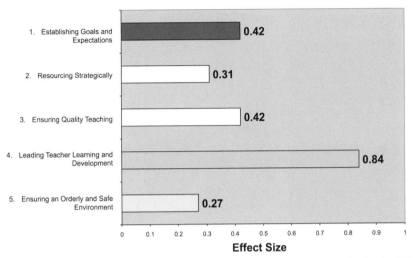

Source: Viviane Robinson, Student-Centred Leadership

We ran a pilot in the summer term of 2015 where Mark Bindon (Vice Principal, Teaching and Learning), Nichole Sanders (Assistant Principal, Staff Development and Sixth Form) and myself coached six colleagues weekly. It was obvious very quickly that a weekly in-class coaching session followed up by another coaching session was having a big impact. TLAC strategies were the usual focus of the coaching conversations.

Since September 2015 every member of teaching staff at Torquay Academy has had weekly coaching. We developed our own approach to coaching using the model outlined by Paul Bambrick-Santoyo in his outstanding book *Leverage Leadership*. The ASAP model on the next page outlines the steps involved in coaching at Torquay Academy.

ASAP Coaching Model

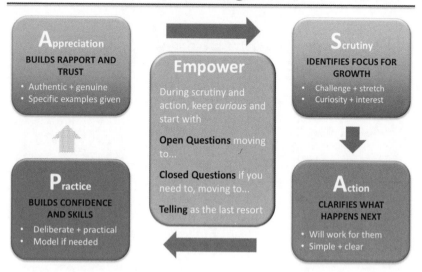

All of our coaches are either part of our Lead Practitioner team or a member of SLT. Each week coaching will start with a 20-minute in-class observation by the coach; this provides the basis for the follow-up coaching conversation. The 20-minute coaching conversation, which takes place in the same week, begins with Appreciation, where the coach highlights a real positive from what was seen. It quickly moves onto Scrutiny, which is the key part of the conversation. The teacher is asked to identify what the action step for the next lesson should be. If the coachee isn't able to quickly suggest an action step, it will be up to the coach to identify one. The action step is a simple and clear development in teaching that can be implemented during the next lesson. The coachee records it in their coaching booklet. The rest of the coaching session is spent practising the action step. This may involve the coach modelling it, but the key is that the teacher will not be carrying out the action step for the first time live in front of a class. The benefits of practice are detailed below in the CPD section.

Coaches record all of the action steps in a centralised document that allows an overview of the techniques that staff are currently developing. The document has the following headings:

- Date in class
- Lesson room
- Action step and date agreed
- Action step progress
- In-class coaching notes

This coaching initiative is a significant investment of time and money by the school, but it is paying great dividends.

> **KEY POINT**
>
> The impact of our coaching is that every teacher at Torquay Academy improves every week.

Coaching of leaders

We also understand the importance of coaching conversations with leaders in the school. 121 leadership meetings (see Leadership at all Levels chapter for more details) will often adopt a coaching approach to conversations. We use the BASIC model of coaching that was developed by Andy Buck.

BASIC Coaching Model

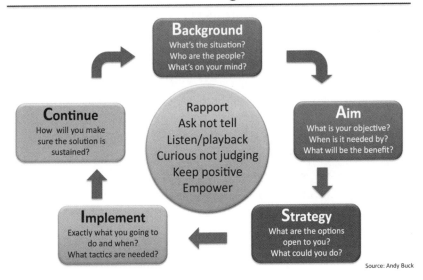

Source: Andy Buck

Professional development

Our budget for professional development is ring-fenced as we all strive to improve as teachers.

We start each academic year with a Teaching and Learning Conference at a local hotel. This event enables us to spend time on the priorities that we want to focus on at the start of the year. All sessions are run by our own staff as we believe we have the expertise within our school. Having the conference in an external venue enables our staff to concentrate on the day and not be distracted by the tasks that await them in their workrooms.

A number of staff, including myself, have attended a variety of Train the Trainer workshops, allowing us to deliver TLAC training in our own school. We are provided with brilliant resources (developed by Doug, Colleen Driggs, Erica Woolway and the rest of the team) that we can adapt. Using these materials, we have been able to deliver INSET of the highest quality, which has had a demonstrable impact in the classroom.

We have a 2.5-hour twilight six times through the year, once per half term. The focus of these twilights is always improving teaching. The training sessions are underpinned by our use of practice. The principles of practice are contained in another of Doug's books, *Practice Perfect*. We have taken note of the key points about practice, namely that it should:

- be carefully designed and planned to get the best results.
- feed back on your performance – when used effectively, practice can give you immediate feedback on your performance.
- yield success; you feel the difference – practising successfully is palpable: you can feel the difference.
- give you a model of excellence – when effective coaches facilitate practice, they will also provide you with a model of what excellence looks like.
- have a cultural/social element – in the context of teaching, practice turns teaching into a team sport.

We practise TLAC techniques during the twilights (and the coaching sessions). This gives our teachers the opportunity to practise those techniques before 'going live' with them in the classroom. This led to some initial embarrassment, but it passed quickly, and colleagues now practise with great enthusiasm and smile as they do it. We understood that TLAC techniques wouldn't make their way into our classrooms simply by having copies of *Teach Like a Champion* and its associated workbook scattered around the school.

KEY POINT

If you want teachers to implement something in the classroom, you should give them the time to practise it before expecting them to do it in front of students for the first time.

These INSET sessions are the most effective training sessions I have taken part in. On the day after we practise a technique, I can hear teachers implementing it in classroom after classroom as I walk around the school.

The best practice videos included in the TLAC training were based in US schools, predominantly Uncommon Schools. One question we were often asked by our colleagues was: could these techniques work in our own classrooms? To demonstrate how TLAC could be successful in Torquay Academy, we set about producing our own videos for the training sessions. Showing our own teachers delivering TLAC techniques in our own classrooms was extremely powerful. All of our resources and videos are shared on our in-house CPD website.

To build capacity in our ability to train our teachers, we set about establishing a team of Lead Practitioners. This team was made up of highly experienced and expert teachers whose role is focused on improving the quality of teaching within the school. This team set about leading training sessions and building up our collection of TLAC videos.

Our staff go on very few external INSET courses. It is very rare for anyone to be out of school unless it is an exam board course, Pixl event or an SWTSA Teaching School subject meeting. This enables our teachers to be where they are needed – in front of our students – and we know we are not spending money on substandard INSET.

Teacher workload

Teaching is hard work. Teaching at Torquay Academy is hard work; we have the highest expectations of every member of our school community. But there are several things we do to try to reduce workload and stress pressures:

- Clear behaviour policy where poor behaviour is never tolerated. Teachers can focus on teaching (the reason they came into our wonderful profession).
- Centralised planning to ensure teachers aren't responsible for planning every lesson they teach.
- No written reports.
- Centralised detentions.
- Written feedback is only given where required.
- Centralised homework means it doesn't have to be thought of, set, collected, and marked for each lesson.
- Coaching and CPD enable you to become a better teacher.
- Teaching your subject specialism.

One of our excellent Lead Practitioners, Kathrine Mortimore, wrote an article for The Guardian outlining how we have found ways to reduce the workload burden on teachers. You can read it at bit.ly/TAguardian

Key action points

- ☐ Are you happy with all of the staff in your school? If not, what are you doing about them?
- ☐ Does your in-house professional development have an impact on student outcomes? If it doesn't, you should carefully assess its value.
- ☐ What is the impact of external professional development? Does it have a positive impact or is it an expensive day out with an average lunch?
- ☐ Are staff given the opportunity to practise ideas that are expected to be implemented in the classroom?

☐ Are there aspects of the job that can be removed from your teachers' workloads?

☐ Do you give enough time for your teachers to improve?

☐ Can you see the impact of your CPD in the classrooms?

Ideas you can implement in your school

☐ A trial group can be set up to see if coaching has a positive impact in your school.

☐ How do you grow your leaders? Would they benefit more from a coaching (rather than mentoring) approach?

The curriculum

Teaching and Learning Cycles

We have divided the academic year into four Teaching and Learning Cycles of nine weeks each. Every subject and year group follows this cycle of seven weeks of teaching, followed by an assessment week and a superteaching week.

Summer Holiday					
			5.9.18	TA way	
	1	A	10.9.18	Teaching	
Autumn Term 7 Weeks	2	B	17.9.18		
	3	A	24.9.18		
	4	B	1.10.18		
	5	A	8.10.18		
	6	B	15.10.18		
Half Term					
	7	A	29.10.18	Teaching	
	8	B	5.11.18		
	1	A	12.11.18	Assessment	
Autumn Term 8 Weeks	1	B	19.11.18	Super Teaching	
	1	A	26.11.18	Teaching	
	2	B	3.12.18		
	3	A	10.12.18		
	4	B	17.12.18		
Christmas					
	5	A	7.1.19	Teaching	
	6	B	14.1.19		
Spring Term 6 Weeks	7	A	21.1.19		
	1	B	28.1.19	Assessment	
	1	A	4.2.19	Super Teaching	
	1	B	11.2.19	Teaching	
Half Term					
	2	A	25.2.19	Teaching	
	3	B	4.3.19		
Spring Term 6 Weeks	4	A	11.3.19		
	5	B	18.3.19		
	6	A	25.3.19		
	7	B	1.4.19		
Easter					
	1	A	22.4.19	Assessment	
Summer Term 5 Weeks	1	B	29.4.19	Super Teaching	
	1	A	6.5.19	Teaching	
	2	A	13.5.19		
	3	B	20.5.19		
Half Term					
	4	A	3.6.19	Teaching	
	5	B	10.6.19		
Summer Term 7 Weeks	6	A	17.6.19		
	7	B	24.6.19		
	1	A	1.7.19	Synoptic Assessment	
	1	B	8.7.19	Super Teaching	
	1	-	15.7.19	Activities Week	

Each cycle starts with students putting an A5 green sticker into their books that identifies what they will be learning over the following seven weeks. Lessons are then taught to ensure that these topics are covered and that students are ready for their exams. The following is an example of what is printed on a green sticker.

KS4 Mathematics
Quarter Topic Sheet
Year 10 Quarter 1

Assessment
Week 8

Your revision
starts now!

By the end of the Cycle I will know I have progress if I can:	Taught	Mid Cycle			End of Cycle		
Topic (Mathswatch clip in brackets)		R	A	G	R	A	G
List different sampling techniques (152, 176)							
Draw a cumulative frequency graphs (186)							
Draw a box plot (187)							
Calculate frequency density and draw a histogram (205)							
Solve quadratic equations by factorisation (157)							
Solve quadratic equations by using the formula (191)							
Solve linear simultaneous equations (140, 162, 211)							
Solve linear inequalities (138, 139)							

TORQUAY ACADEMY **ASPIRE & ACHIEVE**

KEY POINT

The teaching and learning cycles have given the school a real sense of urgency. Lessons are always part of the preparation for an exam in the near future.

In the eighth week of their cycle, students complete the assessment for that quarter. These assessments are made up of multiple-choice questions that test knowledge across the breadth of the teaching cycle. Multiple-choice questions, when well devised, can be very effective at identifying a student's misconceptions. In the second, third and fourth cycle of the year, assessments include questions to re-test material from previous cycles; the synoptic portion of the assessments are 20%, 35% and 50% respectively.

Question level analysis follows the end-of-cycle assessments to pinpoint the areas that individuals or groups have struggled with. The completion and analysis of these tests must not overwhelm the students or staff. The speed of turnaround and the quality of the analysis are key to the success of the assessments and leaders support this turnaround – 48 hours is the target – by clearing the calendar of other commitments. Also, technologies – such as a smartphone app – are being trialled to automatically mark multiple-choice assessments.

Once teachers have carried out a question level analysis, they are able to identify areas for the superteaching week in the ninth week of the cycle (review meetings are covered in the next chapter). This involves structured delivery of the knowledge that students haven't grasped and may involve re-grouping students so that those with similar needs are taught together.

Torquay Academy T&L Cycles

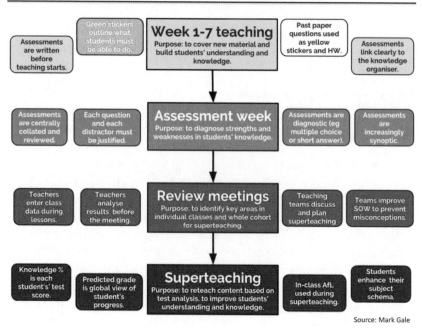

Source: Mark Gale

Marking

During the seven teaching weeks in each cycle, teachers use a wide range of formative assessment approaches to identify gaps in knowledge and understanding. One of those methods is the marking of students' written work.

Twice per learning cycle, students will have a piece of work marked in detail by their teacher. As part of the feedback, the teacher will identify for the student a 'www' (what went well) and an 'ebi' (even better if). Based upon the 'ebi', the teacher will set an activity for the student to enable them to rectify a weakness. All of this is done with a green pen on a yellow sticker. Students then complete the activity in a purple pen. Teachers then check this work with a green pen.

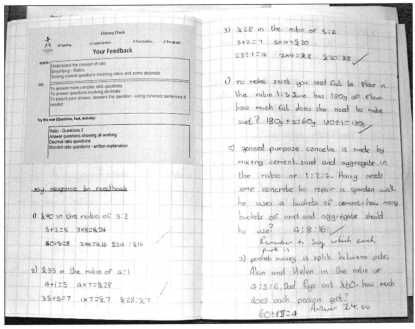

We have started trialling whole-class marking where themes for improvement are reported back to the group.

The curriculum

We have made many appointments as the school has grown and teachers have left us. This has enabled us to shape the curriculum to meet the needs of our students rather than having to fit a historical staffing list. Decisions about recruitment were made based on the curriculum we felt matched the needs of our girls and boys. For us that meant a focus on maths and English; students in Years 7 to 11 get an hour a day of both subjects. In general terms, we are happy with the curriculum, although we know there will be some tweaks in future years as we would like to give more time to science.

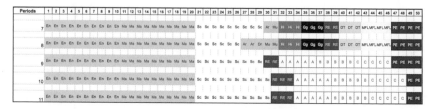

Over the past few years, the school has experienced a rapid increase in student numbers as it moved from being the local sink school to being oversubscribed. Paul Hocking (Assistant Principal, Curriculum) has modelled the curriculum two years in advance, this has enabled us to undertake a full staffing, rooming, and finance analysis of the increase from 820 to 1480 students well ahead of time. This has allowed us to take a proactive approach to all aspects of the curriculum rather than having to make last-minute reactive decisions.

Curriculum design

We need teachers to answer two questions to enable them to design an effective curriculum:

- What do I need to teach for my students to be able to master the questions on the exam?
- How will I know if they have mastered the skills and knowledge required?

Teachers start by designing the assessments that students will face. We believe that unless students and teachers understand how the material taught will be examined, they will always underperform. Experience has demonstrated that lessons too frequently fail because they have been designed backwards, with resources and activities considered first, learning intentions only considered almost as an afterthought. Our cycles are dependent on a clear analysis of the questions posed on the terminal exams, breaking them down into the subject knowledge and skills required to succeed at the highest levels. This leads to expert teachers teaching to the top and fostering an academic passion in their students.

We try to dedicate as much time as possible to enabling our teachers to work collaboratively to develop the curriculum and teaching resources.

Homework

The basis of our homework is that it is set up to improve the knowledge and exam readiness of all students irrespective of the support they have at home. It is transparent, and every student and parent knows what has been set for them at the start of each cycle. It has the effect of boosting students' confidence as the knowledge gained can be used in class. This is reinforced by the use of low-stakes testing and creates a culture where we hope students value knowledge and learning.

Our experience showed us that there was a correlation between supportive parents and the amount of homework a child would do. We wanted to design a system that removed this correlation and ensured that all students would complete high-quality homework that would improve their knowledge and readiness for exams.

The previous homework system created a large burden for teachers as they would be expected to set imaginative tasks that were simply set because that subject appeared on the homework timetable. That work had to be recorded correctly in lessons, checked, marked and sanctions put in place for students who had failed to complete it to a satisfactory standard.

Knowledge organisers – an overhaul of homework

Knowledge organisers contain the basic knowledge needed to underpin the learning during each cycle and to be successful in their lessons and ultimately the assessment. They can also then be used as revision tools shortly before the end of cycle tests.

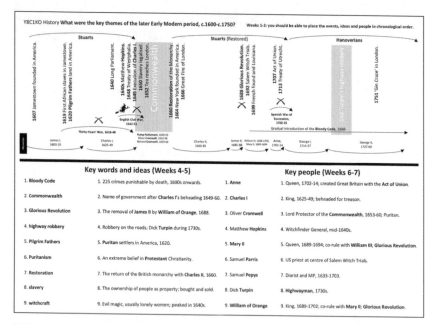

We run sessions for each year group to explain how they should be using the knowledge organisers – essentially an adapted version of look, cover, write. Students are given a pack containing the knowledge organisers for every subject, a practice book and plastic wallet to keep them in.

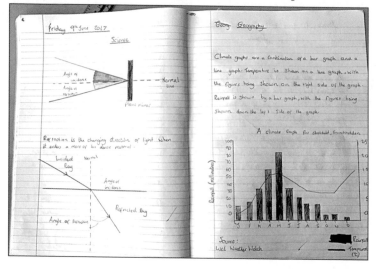

In Years 7 and 8, students do four 20-minute homework assignments every night. These are predominantly based on their knowledge organisers, but there are some variations for maths and English; there are some online maths tasks and reading four nights a week.

As GCSE courses begin in Year 9, we had to extend the homework to include GCSE questions.

The homework expectations for Key Stage 4 are 1 hour and 30 minutes per evening, Monday to Thursday, and 1 hour and 40 minutes on a Friday. Each evening's homework consists of a 30-minute examination question and 3 × 20 minutes of revision from knowledge organisers (apart from Friday where there are two examination questions and two knowledge organisers).

Homework Years 9-11 90 minutes per evening					
	Monday	Tuesday	Wednesday	Thursday	Fri/Sat/ Sun
Exam Question **30 mins**	English	Maths	Science	Option A	Option B Option C
Revision Knowledge Organiser 20 mins	Maths	Option C	RS	Option A	
Revision Knowledge Organiser 20 mins	Option B	English	Maths	Option C	Science
Revision Knowledge Organiser 20 mins	Option A	Science	Option B	English	Maths

Instead of homework practice books, students use seven-part folders, one section for each subject. These folders are filled with examination questions and knowledge organisers for each subject on the first day of each quarter.

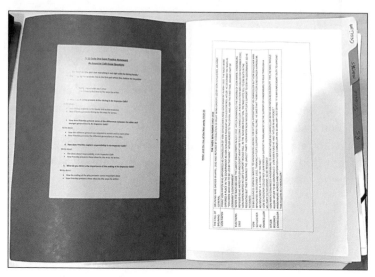

In Key Stage 4, students choose how to use their knowledge organisers. They are taught three methods of revision, and they choose the one they find most suitable for them. Materials, such as note cards, folders, and books, are given to them to assist them with their homework.

There is transparency in the system for students, parents and staff as all homework is issued on the first day of each new learning cycle. It also has the benefit for the staff of reducing workload as the knowledge organiser homework does not need to be marked. Only the GCSE examination questions need to be reviewed; often this will be done via peer assessment or walking talking marking (where the teacher marks a piece of work while explaining where marks are awarded on the visualiser).

All homework is checked in the morning by the form tutors. Punishments for non-completion are handled centrally, meaning classroom teachers do not have to set detentions or chase students for non-attendance.

There has been a significant increase in independent study, which can be seen around the school every day. One particular example that raised eyebrows with local schools was when our boys who were competing in a rugby 7s tournament took out their knowledge organisers and practice books in between matches!

Literacy support

Former Assistant Principal Leigh Withers has overseen a comprehensive programme that seeks to eliminate literacy as a barrier to learning. The literacy programme has seen some stunning results: the average increase in reading age for all students during Years 7 and 8 is over five years.

All students are tested on their first day in Year 7 to provide baseline data. This is used in conjunction with other information to determine those students who will need additional support. The interventions we run are primarily based on Read Write Inc., Lexia and Achieve.

During form time, all of Year 7 and 8 read a classic text with their tutor. Year 7 pupils have read *The Time Machine* by H G Wells and Pride and Prejudice by Jane Austen; and the Year 8s have read Wuthering Heights by Emily Bronte and *Journey to the Centre of the Earth* by Jules Verne.

In addition to this, our KS3 pupils have their own specific Reading Record. This record contains a table of books that the student needs to read over the year. The books are selected to ensure that students are stretched by taking into account their reading age. Within this list, there is a classic novel and a text from another culture.

Effective use of tutor time

Once the equipment check has been completed the rest of the 20-minute tutor time is used to support learning. Each year group has an assembly one morning a week, leaving four mornings to be filled. In Years 7 and 8, students complete numeracy tasks one morning a week, and they read a classic novel together for the other three. Year 9s use the time to support their homework. Years 10 and 11 are placed in tutor groups with core subject teachers where they spend 20 minutes a day revising, recapping key concepts, or developing exam technique.

KEY POINT

Every second counts when the students are in school. Using tutor time to support learning can add days to your contact time each year.

The school day

Students are expected to be in school by 8.20am ready to line up and walk into the school building at 8.27am. We have five 1-hour lessons:

Registration/Assembly: 8.30 – 8.50am

Period 1: 8.50 – 9.50am

Period 2: 9.50 – 10.50am

BREAK: 10.50 – 11.15am

Period 3: 11.15 – 12.15pm

Period 4: 12.15 – 1.15pm

LUNCH: 1.15 – 2.00pm

Period 5: 2.00 – 3.00pm

Extended day

Every teacher undertakes a period 6 lesson – this is an additional hour at the end of the school day. We run period 6 for our Year 11s and 13s, but also for other year groups when the superteaching week isn't sufficient time to overcome misunderstandings. This requires separate timetabling, and this is overseen by Owen Gratton (SLE and Academic Intervention).

During the run-up to examinations, after-school sessions are extended to two and a half hours for the groups of students who require additional learning time.

Extracurricular

In addition to the academic extended day, there are many activities on offer to our students; this forms part of Assistant Principal Gareth Harries's oversight. The majority of the opportunities are sporting or creative arts. Our Performing Arts Academy offers students who are talented in music, singing and dance to have access to professional instructors for four hours a week.

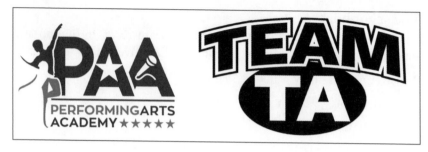

Key action points

- ☐ Are students clear about when their next assessment will be? Do they know what knowledge they will need to pass the test?
- ☐ How do you identify the students' areas of misunderstanding and what is done to rectify these?
- ☐ Is there clarity in the marking policy? Do staff and students know what is expected of them?
- ☐ Does the curriculum in every year group support outcomes at 16 and 18?
- ☐ Audit the homework that is being set. Is it of sufficient quantity and quality? Does it support the students' learning?
- ☐ How are students who require literacy support identified? How are any weaknesses overcome?
- ☐ Observe what is taking place during tutor time at the moment.

Ideas you can implement in your school

- ☐ Provide a clear annual timetable of when assessments will take place. Share this with parents and carers.
- ☐ Undertake question level analysis of assessments in all year groups.
- ☐ Provide parents with copies of the homework timetable and ensure they know how to find what homework has been set.
- ☐ Change how tutor time is used to support the students' learning. Placing English and maths teachers as your Year 11 tutors is a straightforward way of starting this.

Data analysis

'The definition of insanity is doing the same thing over and over and expecting different results.'
Unknown

Knowing your students' and the school's next steps are the key to improvement.

Student data analysis

Key Stages 4 and 5

Data is collected at the end of every quarter. Subject teachers report fine level predicted grades for Key Stages 4 and 5. Teachers don't make their predictions in isolation; they are discussed and justified in subject areas to improve accuracy. The fine grades reflect the degree of confidence the teacher has in the student getting that grade:

- 4+ = secure at grade 4 but needs intervention to achieve a grade 5
- 4 = insecure – needs intervention to secure a grade 4
- 4– = insecure – as likely to get a grade 3, needs intervention

Mark Gale (Assistant Principal, Narrowing the Gaps) oversees the manipulation and analysis of this data. GCSE data is analysed using SISRA, and we produce a RAISE document after each quarter. A level data is uploaded to ALPs connect. This allows for in-depth analysis by senior and middle leaders, as well as classroom teachers. Every teacher also receives a bespoke data sheet (Atkinson reports) for their class after every quarter that helps them to identify gaps and to focus on students who need to improve to meet their target grades.

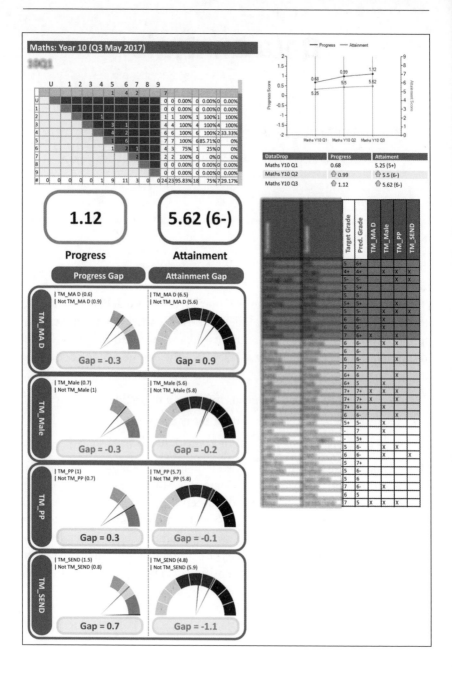

GCSE targets are based upon Key Stage 2 results. 1.33 grades are added to the Department for Education's expected grades; this is where our Pygmalion cycle of the highest expectations begins. While these targets may appear to be fiercely ambitious, in 2016 one-third of our students achieved these targets in every subject.

We have a relentless focus on progress. Evan Pugh (Vice Principal Student Progress) oversees this drive to ensure that every student achieves their target grades. He oversees our war boards around the school. One example of this is in my meeting room where the walls are covered with student pictures (our war boards). GCSE students are placed on the board plotting their target grades (Key Stage 2 scores) against their predicted progress score. This is a very useful tool for us in having our students' progress in front of us every day. It also means we have all the data needed when meeting with staff or students.

The workrooms in each of the learning areas also have their own war boards that visualise the progress of students in their own subjects.

In the sixth form, we use ALPs to set targets for A-levels and BTECs. ALPs reports are run after each quarter to enable in-depth analysis.

Key Stage 3

At Key Stage 3, we have adopted our own life-after-levels system where knowledge and skills are separated. Skills develop gradually over the Key Stage while knowledge may be more erratic as topics of varying difficulty are studied. We would therefore expect the skills score to increase gradually over time, but the knowledge score may show a spikier profile over time. The increase in a student's skill score enables us to demonstrate the progress the student is making over time.

The knowledge score is recorded as a simple percentage. The skill score is recorded on a scale of 1–25.

Each subject has identified key skills that students need to develop in readiness for GCSE and A level study, for example, use of Scientific Models, Analysis of Historical Sources or Evaluating a Process or Product in Technology. These skills are split into five increasingly demanding bands with scores of 1–5, 6–10, 11–15, 16–20 and 21–25. Within each of these bands, the score students receive depends upon whether they *rarely, occasionally, often, generally*, or *consistently* meet that skill.

	1 - 5	6 - 10	11 - 15	16 - 20	21 - 25
	Rarely Occasionally Often Generally Consistently	Rarely Occasionally Often Generally Consistently	Rarely Occasionally Often Generally Consistently	Rarely Occasionally Often Generally Consistently	Rarely Occasionally Often Generally Consistently
Scientific ideas and models	Use simple models to describe scientific ideas. Contrast scientific ideas and non-scientific ideas.	Use abstract models to describe scientific ideas. Recognise scientific questions that do not yet have definitive answers.	Identify strengths and weaknesses of different models. Explain how new scientific evidence is discussed by the scientific community.	Clearly use multi-step abstract models to explain scientific phenomena. Explain how evidence supports accepted scientific ideas or contributes to questions that science cannot answer.	Explain processes or phenomena logically and in detail making use of abstract ideas and models from different areas of science. Analyse the development of scientific theories over time.
The impact of science on society	Recognise simple positive and negative consequences of scientific developments. Recognise applications of specific scientific ideas. Identify aspects of science used in particular jobs.	Describe different viewpoints about scientific developments. Identify ethical or moral issues related to scientific developments. Link applications of science to their underpinning scientific ideas.	Describe how different decisions on the uses of science may be made in different contexts. Describe how scientific developments have provided evidence to pose further questions. Describe how aspects of science are applied in particular jobs.	Explain how scientific discoveries can change worldviews. Suggest ethical, moral, social, cultural or economic arguments for and against scientific developments. Explain how creative thinking generates ideas for future scientific research.	Evaluate the effects of scientific developments on society as a whole. Explain the unintended consequences that may arise from scientific developments.
Scientific communication	Present simple scientific data in more than one way, including bar charts and tables. Use scientific forms of language in simple contexts.	Select appropriate ways of presenting scientific data. Use appropriate scientific forms of language to communicate scientific ideas, processes and phenomena.	Distinguish between opinion and scientific evidence. Decide on the most appropriate formats to present data, such as line graphs for continuous variables. Distinguish between data from primary and secondary sources.	Identify lack of balance in the presentation of evidence, and any areas of incompleteness. Use language as a scientist would, including key vocabulary and structure.	Represent abstract ideas using appropriate symbols, flow diagrams and graphs. Present robust and well-structured explanations, arguments and counter-arguments verbally and in writing.
Scientific investigations	Identify control variables. Make some accurate observations. Recognise obvious risks when prompted.	Explain how factors are being controlled to carry out a fair test. Make sets of observations, identifying the ranges and intervals used. Identify possible risks.	Recognise variables in investigations, selecting the most suitable to investigate. Repeat observations when appropriate, selecting suitable ranges and intervals. Control obvious risks.	Identify significant variables and recognise which are independent and dependent. Justify choices of method, range and intervals. Recognise and control a range familiar risks.	Formulate hypotheses that can be investigated. Identify key variables in complex contexts, explain why some may be uncontrollable and plan appropriate approaches to take this into account. Complete a risk assessment, using suitable information.
Analysis and evaluation of scientific data	Identify straightforward patterns in observations or data presented in various formats. Describe what has been found out in investigations, linking cause and effect. Suggest improvements to working methods.	Identify patterns in data presented in various formats, including line graphs. Draw conclusions based on scientific knowledge. Suggest improvements to working methods, giving reasons.	Recognise and explain differences in repeated observations. Draw valid conclusions that utilise more than one piece of supporting evidence, including numerical data and line graphs. Evaluate the effectiveness of working methods, making practical suggestions to improve them.	Draw conclusions that are consistent with the evidence and explain them using scientific knowledge. Make valid comments on the quality of data. Explain how data can be interpreted in different ways.	Use quantitative relationships between variables to inform conclusions and further predictions. Assess the strength of evidence, deciding if it is sufficient to support a conclusion. Explain ways of modifying working methods to improve reliability of data.
Approx NC level	3B → 4C	4B → 5C	5B → 6C	6B → 7C	7B → 8A
Expected GCSE grade in Y11:	1-2 G-F	3-4 E-D	4-5 D-C	6-7 B-A	8-9 A*

These skill marks are averaged to give an overall subject skill from 1–25.

English ▼		7Q/En1 ▼	Quarter 4 ▼	Click here for SIMS export		Score Q4	Ave Q4	Ave Q3	Ave Q2	Ave Q1
English		1 2 3 4 5 6 7 8 9 10 11 12 13 14 15 16 17 18 19 20 21 22 23 24 25								
FAWLTY Basil	Reading response	Q1 Q2 Q3 Q4				10				
	Evaluating writer's craft	Q1 Q2 Q3 Q4				9	8.8	8.4	7.4	7.0
	Relationship between texts and contexts	Q1 Q2 Q3 Q4				8				
End of year target	Writing content and organisation	Q1 Q2 Q3 Q4				8				
9	Technical accuracy	Q1 Q2 Q3 Q4				9				

Key Stage 2 data is used to give students a target skill score from 1–25.

Knowledge is reported as a percentage in the most recent assessment for each subject at the end of the teaching cycle. This score may go up and down across cycles: students' knowledge in different topics will not necessarily be equal.

Reflection meetings

We hold assessment review meetings on the Monday after assessment week. By this time, all staff have marked and analysed the tests for each of their classes. The HOLA leads the meeting for their learning area. Staff discuss the outcomes of each test and plan the superteaching week lessons by identifying the topics that need re-teaching. It is possible to identify if any of these areas are an issue across the year group or isolated to specific classes.

They also note where and how the scheme of work could be improved by looking at lessons covering content that students did not perform well on.

Because all seven year groups have to be covered in the same meeting, only about ten minutes can be allocated to each test review. All the teachers of these classes participate in the discussion; it is beneficial for teachers to see and hear the reviews of other year groups' assessments.

We offer guidance to support effective teacher reflection meetings:

Before the meeting
- Ensure that the assessments have been marked.

   Diagnostic assessments (multiple choice or single-word answers) are easy to mark, can be processed instantly, and give clear information about strengths and weaknesses.

- Ensure that results from all classes are collated into one place. This could be a departmental Google sheet.

- Use question level analysis (QLA) to identify which questions caused difficulties for your class and/or the whole cohort.

At the meeting
- Go through the questions, particularly agreeing which ones need to be addressed during superteaching.

  Refer to the data ('Only 25% of students got this question right', or 'Only 10% of my students got it right, while 70% of the whole cohort got it right') rather than hunches ('My class seemed to get on well with this topic').

- Once questions and topics are identified, decide:
  - Do they need a superteaching lesson or part of one? Allocate staff to prepare these.
  - Should they feature as regular low stakes Do Now questions? Allocate staff to add them to the bank of Do Now questions.

- Note the topics that need to be addressed on the form in the HOLA leadership file, so that schemes of work and resources can be amended to help prevent similar issues with the next cohort.

After the meeting
- Make sure that the meetings allocated in subsequent weeks to altering the last quarter's materials are used to address the issues raised during the Teacher Reflection meeting.

KEY POINT

Schools collect vast amounts of data on their students. How do you use this to improve their learning?

Reporting to parents

Results are reported to parents at the end of every quarter. Key Stage 4 and 5 students' parents are given target and predicted grades for each subject, and the percentage mark from the assessment. No written comments are provided unless the student is below target in a particular subject; in that case, the subject teacher explains why they are below target and what the student can do to get back on target. Students also receive separate effort grades for mindset for learning and behaviour for each subject plus an overall effort grade for their attendance and homework.

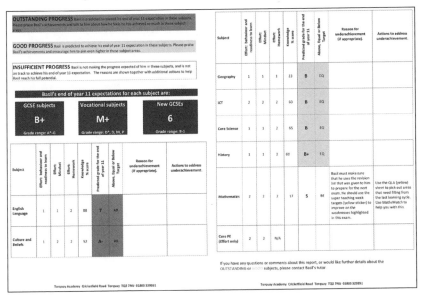

Ranking students

At the end of each quarter, we rank each student based on their effort during the previous quarter. An average grade is calculated based on a student's attendance, behaviour and readiness to learn, the mindset for learning, and homework. Effort grades are then placed into different bands based upon university degree classifications: from first class to third class and unclassified. There is transparency in how to achieve top effort grades; posters, like the one on the next page, are placed around the school.

How to achieve 1st Class Effort
With hard work, there are no limits

Academy attendance effort	1	100% attendance.
	2	96 – 99% attendance.
	3	92 – 95% – Requires Improvement.
	4	Below 92% – Unsatisfactory.

Behaviour and readiness to learn	1	Outstanding behaviour. Always brings all the correct equipment.
	2	Good behaviour. Brings the correct equipment and is ready to learn.
	3	Behaviour requires improvement or does not always bring the correct equipment.
	4	Unsatisfactory behaviour or rarely brings the correct equipment.

Mindset for learning	1	Fully committed to getting the most out of learning by being curious, actively seeking feedback, reacting to failure by trying harder and thriving on challenge. Work produced shows outstanding effort.
	2	A hard-working student who shows resilience, uses feedback and criticism to improve and challenges themselves in lessons. Work produced shows good effort.
	3	Does what is expected, but only sometimes challenges themselves in lessons. Uses feedback to try to improve, but does not always show resilience. The amount of effort shown in work requires an improvement.
	4	Does not challenge themselves in lesson or respond well to feedback. Switches off if something is too hard. Unsatisfactory effort shown in work.

Homework	1	Always completes homework on time and challenges themselves to complete high quality work or extension tasks.
	2	Always completes homework on time to a good standard.
	3	Sometimes completes homework on time but quality of homework requires improvement.
	4	Unsatisfactory - rarely or never completes homework.

TORQUAY
ACADEMY
In aspire and to achieve

The ranked lists are then placed in the main atrium of the school. There is always great interest from the students who want to know what has happened to their average score and their ranking in the year group.

Key action points

- ☐ Are full written reports for each subject a good use of your teachers' time?
- ☐ What grades do staff report to you: current or predicted? Can you justify your choice?
- ☐ How do you ensure data collections have an impact on the students' learning? Does it lead to intervention to ensure gaps in knowledge are corrected?

Ideas you can implement in your school

- ☐ Fine grades enable teachers to highlight which students are in need of intervention to secure grades.
- ☐ Having war boards in department spaces will ensure all teachers will be aware of the key students in their subject area.
- ☐ Ranking students by their effort can give a very powerful message.

Leadership at all levels

'Never doubt that a small group of thoughtful and committed people can change the world.'
President Bartlet, *The West Wing*

We are blessed with an incredible team of leaders at all levels. They work tirelessly to improve the school and ensure that everyone succeeds. All leaders know they can't unsee something and they act with great strength and moral purpose to effect change and secure excellence.

SLT

We have built what many would describe as a large SLT. First, they are all exceptional teachers (they have a teaching load of 15–25 hours per week); beyond that, they all have a narrow area of responsibility which they can devote all of their energies to. Having a large team who are able to devote their time to a small number of given areas was essential given the amount of change we needed to implement. The makeup of our SLT is as follows:

- Principal
- Vice Principal – Teaching & Learning
- Vice Principal – Progress & Attainment
- Principal Finance Director
- Assistant Principal – Behaviour & Alternative Provision
- Assistant Principal – Narrowing the Gap
- Assistant Principal – Extracurricular & external relations
- Assistant Principal – Curriculum
- Assistant Principal – SEND
- Assistant Principal – Sixth Form and Staff Development
- Assistant Principal – Maths Progress

- Designated Safeguarding Officer
- SLE – Academic Intervention

When I read Katzenbach and Smith's definition of a team, from *The Wisdom of Teams*, I see our SLT: a 'group of people with complementary skills who are committed to a common purpose, performance goals and approach for which they are mutually accountable'.

Morning briefings

SLT meet for 10–15 minutes four mornings a week. This provides us with the opportunity to share any news, issues, or concerns that we have. This has proved to be essential in keeping the whole team on the same page, moving forwards and avoiding potential issues. Many operational issues are dealt with at this meeting.

On the other morning, there is an alternating cycle of briefings. One week there are two briefings: one for SLT and HOLAs (Heads of Learning Areas) and the other for SLT and Progress Leaders. On the next week, the Progress Leaders meet with their tutor teams.

We have a whole-staff briefing once a week on a Monday morning for 10 minutes.

SLT meetings

There is a weekly 80-minute meeting scheduled for SLT. The meetings follow a nine-week rotation in line with the T&L cycles:

1. Full SLT
2. SLT working parties
3. Full SLT
4. SMLT
5. Full SLT
6. SLT working parties
7. Full SLT
8. SMLT
9. Principal priority

Full SLT

We use this meeting to discuss strategic and operational issues. There are a number of standing items are always discussed:

- Year 11
- Year 13
- Teaching and learning
- Events in the next three weeks

The agenda is held in a shared appointment in our Google calendar. Anyone is free to add agenda items to the meeting. The Chair is rotated each meeting, and it is up to them to ensure that each item is given the appropriate duration – and that the meeting finishes on time!

We don't record minutes of the meeting, just outcomes using the following template.

	Subject	Action	Lead person	Date to be achieved by
1				

SLT working parties

The SLT is divided into smaller groups who each work collectively on achieving a key objective from the three-year plan. This meeting gives the team the time they need to effect the necessary change to continue driving the school forwards.

We meet for 15 minutes at the end of the meeting to feed back to the wider SLT about how the projects are going and what they are planning next.

SMLT working parties

Our Senior and Middle Leadership Team is a real powerhouse of the school. This group has implemented many aspects of school improvement and has become a real driving force for improvement. Each SMLT group is led by a non-SLT colleague, and they work upon an area of interest.

The area each group is working on was decided by everyone making suggestions about the areas we felt the school could improve upon. We then used Amit Varma's tool to rank each of the identified areas based on the size of impact and the ease of implementation.

Prioritising

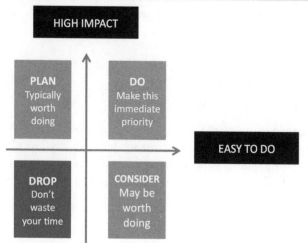

Source: Amit Varma

Each of the areas was then ranked as either Do, Plan, Consider or Drop. This enabled us to have a clear rationale for choosing particular areas to work upon.

Principal priority

This provides a degree of flexibility to me enabling us to meet as required at that time. We also use this meeting to update each other on what our three action points will be before the next T&L cycle.

SLT seminar

Each year the SLT use a weekend towards the end of June to engage in strategic planning. This is an invaluable date in the year that allows us to get many things in place for the following year. Each SLT seminar starts with a State of the Nation overview that allows me to reflect on the highs and lows of the previous 12 months.

Each member of SLT then has three minutes to present the key aspects of their impact over the past year. This is then written up into a case study which we collate into a document that presents an overview of the year's work which is published and made available on our website, bit.ly/TAdocuments.

We have a metaphor based upon a film for each seminar with each member of SLT taking on a character from that film. You'll find the posters produced over the past few years in SLT offices. While they always raise a smile, they provide a reminder of where we were at that point in time.

2014

This was our first SLT seminar, and it was a new team. Along with it came a rip-off of the poster that was in every student's room during my university days. This was about our leadership and how we would effect change. We spent time defining the TA brand and what it means to us, writing a new SEF and exploring Kotter's 8 stage process of creating change. We used the template below to map out key changes that we were planning to implement.

Implementing change – the change from the AIP is:

"

"

Step 1: Establishing a Sense of Urgency	
Step 2: Creating the Guiding Coalition	
Step 3: Developing a Change Vision	
Step 4: Communicating the Vision for Buy-in	
Step 5: Empowering Broad-based Action	
Step 6: Generating Short-term Wins	
Step 7: Never Letting Up	
Step 8: Incorporating Changes into the Culture	

2015

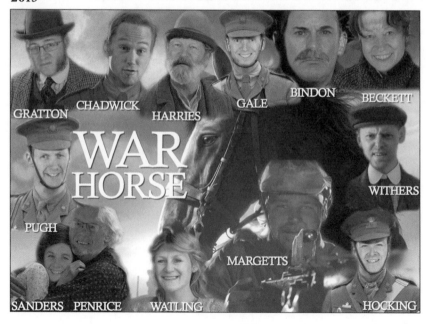

In *War Horse*, the machine gun changed everything. This was the year we introduced coaching, and I believed it would change everything for us.

2016

'Ladies and gentlemen, you are the top 1% of all teachers – the elite, the BEST of the best. We'll make you better. Have an in-class coaching session with a follow-up meeting every week, attend twilights and TAPD (Torquay Academy Professional Development). Now in each lesson, you're going to meet a different challenge. Every encounter is going to be much more difficult. We're going to teach you to teach your lessons right to the edge of the envelope, better than you've ever taught before – and more effective. Now, we don't make policy here, ladies and gentlemen. Elected officials, civilians, do that. We are the instruments of that policy. And although we're not being inspected, we must always act as though we are being inspected.'

– Our amended version of Jester's welcome speech to the new recruits to Top Gun.

2017

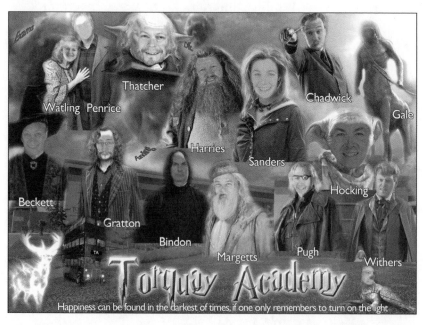

The dementors are everywhere: funding, DfE, Ofsted, examinations… . It is important that we stay focused on what we can control; we must remain positive, and our ambitious targets will not change irrespective of external factors. 'Happiness can be found even in the darkest of times if one only remembers to turn on the light.' – Albus Dumbledore.

Three-year plan

Each year we produce a three-year plan under the following five headings:

- Outcomes – Belief in potential and achievement. Relentless focus on the individual and pushing the boundaries of what they can attain.
- Teaching & Learning and Assessment – Leaders focus their time on supporting teachers to be better teachers.
- Behaviour & Welfare – Students are safe, happy, and driven to learn; they are resilient and focused on achievement.
- Leadership & Management – We believe in the power of leaders at all levels and their potential impact.
- Sixth Form – Unlock and challenge students' potential as they move on to their next phase in life.

Key targets for the following three years are written for each of the five areas. These demonstrate where our efforts will lie in the next year and what we anticipate will be the focus in the two years following that. Each year the three-year plan is rewritten, and previous statements may be amended to reflect how priorities and need change over time. A copy can be found on our website, bit.ly/TAdocuments.

In each of the five areas, we identify one Wildly Important Goal (WIG). The plan is then printed onto a 2m by 4m board and placed in the central atrium of the school.

Continuously improving

3 Year Plan

WIG: Wildly Important Goal

		2017-18	2018-19	2019-20
Outcomes	Belief in potential and achievement. Relentless focus on the individual and pushing the boundaries on what they can attain.	**WIG: 80% 5AC inc. E&M. 0.8 Progress 8.** To remain in the top 1% of schools in the SW for progress. Every student achieves a positive progress 8 score. All subjects above national progress averages.	**WIG: 85% 5AC inc. E&M. 0.9 Progress 8.** To remain in the top 1% of schools in the SW for progress. Every student achieves a positive progress 8 score. All subjects above national progress averages.	**WIG: 90% 5AC inc. E&M. 1.0 Progress 8.** To remain in the top 1% of schools in the SW for progress. Every student achieves a positive progress 8 score. All subjects significantly above national progress averages.
Teaching & Learning and Assessment	Leaders focus their time on supporting teachers to be better teachers.	**WIG: Assessments provide focused feedback upon how to improve.** Coaching is recognised as world class. Practice is central to improvements in T&L. Interventions are effective in supporting students to make progress in all year groups.	**WIG: Assessments are further improved to provide better diagnosis** Interventions ensure substantial and sustained progress. Ensure coaches keep improving. Staff and students have a shared TLAC language of agreed strategies.	**WIG: schemes of work are reappraised to anticipate and prevent students' misconceptions.** Teaching is consistently exceptional (but can still be even better).
Behaviour & Welfare	Students are safe, happy and driven to learn; they are resilient and focus on achievement.	**WIG: Eliminate low level disruption from our classrooms.** Students develop growth mindsets. Extend opportunities within the House system. Attendance to be above national average for each year group. Students develop debating skills and challenge views with an enquiring mind.	**WIG: Low level disruption has been removed from our school.** Embed the House system in the calendar. Students have growth mindsets: resilience and determination. Students are skilled debaters who consider opposing views objectively. Better support for parents to support their child's learning.	**WIG: Students have growth mindsets and approach everything with an ethic of excellence.** Increase in students' cultural capital. School lives and breathes SMSC and British Values.
Leadership & Management	We believe in the power of leaders at all levels and their potential impact.	**WIG: eliminate gaps in progress; focus on MAPP, MA and PP.** Establish use of new self evaluation cycles. Increased number of students getting an all through school experience. Extend involvement in SWTSA networks.	**WIG: peer reviews established.** Relentless pursuit in continuing to eliminate all gaps in progress for all groups. Cross phase systems accelerate progress at TA and feeder schools.	**WIG: peer reviews embedded across school.** There are no gaps in progress and all barriers to learning have been removed. Greater alignment of cross phase systems between TA and feeder schools.
6th Form	Unlock and challenge students' potential as they move on to their next phase in life.	**WIG: Progress to be above the national average.** Retention rates to be above the national average. Increased numbers of students moving on to a Russell Group university. Zero NEETs.	**WIG: Progress to be above the national average for every subject.** Develop students as independent learners. TA university graduates to return and support current students. Increased peer mentoring and tutoring.	**WIG: Progress to be in the top 5% of schools in the SW.** All subjects to remain above national progress averages. Students become leaders in their own right; in school and in the community.

Wildly important goals (WIGs)

We took the language of WIGs from *The 4 Disciplines of Execution* by Chris McChesney, Sean Covey, and Jim Huling. They write that instead of giving mediocre effort to dozens of goals, it is better to focus your finest efforts on the one or two goals that will make all the difference. These are your Wildly Important Goals. Differentiating your WIGs from the day job (they describe this as 'the whirlwind') is about applying more energy to fewer goals.

Having one WIG in each of the areas enables us to identify what we believe is the critical target. This provides a clear message to our community about where our focus will be over the coming year. They are printed and placed all around the school. I do not want our key targets lost in everything else we do.

KEY POINT

Select your WIGs and share them with everyone. You want to ensure everyone is clear about what you feel are the most important things to be working on.

SEF (Self-evaluation form) and improvement plans

We take a relentless approach to school improvement. We have to continually improve: our students deserve it. Our process of self-evaluation and improvement planning is at the heart of what we do.

SEF

An accurate SEF underpins our improvement cycles – it outlines where our school is today. We use it in the same way that we use detailed and accurate student data; knowing exactly where you are enables you to plan the next steps effectively. In Jim Collins's book, Good to Great, he outlines how leaders must confront the brutal facts while maintaining an unwavering faith in future success. We seek out our weaknesses and share them honestly in our SEF. A copy can be found on our website, bit. ly/TAdocuments.

Our SEF opens with a brief introduction/context. This is followed by a section for each of the Ofsted judgements and other key areas. They are:

- Leadership and management
- Teaching, learning, and assessment
- Behaviour and welfare
- Outcomes for pupils
- Sixth form
- English
- Maths
- Pupil premium
- Most able
- Literacy across the curriculum
- Numeracy across the curriculum
- SMSC

For each section, we provide a one-sentence summary and sources of evidence. We then list strengths and areas for development. Judgements are given for each Ofsted area as well as an overall judgement.

The final section of our SEF looks back at previous Ofsted inspections. For each issue brought up by Ofsted, we outline the progress and impact. The benefit of this is twofold: first, we are able to collectively focus upon improving those areas that have been identified by Ofsted; second, it demonstrates to our stakeholders, including governors and Ofsted, that we are acting upon their comments and making an impact.

KEY POINT

The SEF must be an honest reflection of your current strengths and weaknesses. When it is shared with your community, it will enable your leaders to confront the reality of the situation you are in and work towards improving it.

Academy improvement plan (AIP)

The AIP is written ready for the start of a new academic year. There are six sections to the AIP, the five areas of the three-year plan plus any issues that arise from the SEF:

- Outcomes
- Teaching & Learning and Assessment
- Behaviour & Welfare
- Leadership & Management
- Sixth Form
- Issues arising from SEF

Each of the targets from the three-year plan and any issues identified in the SEF are listed as a focus. For each of these, there may be several different actions. Each action has the following points associated with it:

- Group of students to be impacted
- Actions
- Success criteria

- Who
- When

Outcomes – SLT Development Plan 2017-18					
Belief in potential and achievement. Relentless focus on the individual and pushing the boundaries on what they can attain.					
Focus	Group of students to be impacted	Action	Success criteria	Who	When
WIG: 80% 5AC inc. E&M. 0.8 Progress 8.					
To remain in the top 1% of schools in the SW for progress.					
All subjects above national progress averages.					
Every student achieves a positive progress 8 score.					

While the AIP is a very important part of our process of improvement, my frustration with it is that it is out of date as soon as it is written. This is why our improvement process is underpinned by 121s and our nine-week cycle of action planning.

121s

I meet with each member of SLT for an hour every other week for a 121. Members of SLT also meet with the HOLA and Progress Leader they line-manage bi-weekly.

Appointments are shared using our online calendar, and either of us is able to add to the agenda. I find this time is vital as it enables us to work on their strategic goals for the school. We also discuss their 121s with the middle leaders they line-manage. All outcomes are recorded in an online spreadsheet (assigned SLT outcomes are also recorded here) with completion dates, and they are RAGed throughout the year. They are held online, and I am able to access all 121s; this combined with the meetings give me clear lines of sight into all areas of the school. My former headteacher, Roy Pike, once told me, 'I operate on a need-to-know basis and I need to know everything.' 121s are a mix of discussion, coaching, and mentoring.

121s keep our improvement plan alive. These meetings, along with those detailed in the next section, ensure the improvement planning isn't about a document that is written at the start of the year. Improvement planning is continually seeking out improvements and acting upon them. The concept of marginal gains underpins this approach.

Our SLT, with the support of Andy Buck, agreed on what we felt made a great 121. We all attempt to ensure that our 121s adhere to these ten points:

1. Schedule your 121s well in advance, avoid cancelling and turn up on time.

2. Have a shared agenda that either person can add to and add agenda items as early as possible to allow better preparation.

3. The agenda should be a mix of the operational and strategic.

4. Avoid the temptation for the 121 to be an update – this can often be done in other ways. Try to make the 121s about things that need discussion.

5. Ask questions more than you give advice. Make your 121s developmental. Use a coaching approach when you can.

6. You are both accountable for the agreed actions. Stick to agreed timeframes.

7. The meeting doesn't have to be restricted to an office – get out and gather evidence about what you are discussing.

8. Occasionally, ask for help with something you are working on that you would value their opinion or help with.

9. Try to ensure they leave feeling valued, energised, and positive.

10. If you have any follow-up actions, try to do them the same day if you can.

KEY POINT

Finding time to work 121 with the school's leaders enables you to drive the pace of change rapidly forwards.

A nine-week cycle of action planning

HOLAs and Progress Leaders meet with their line managers in weeks 1, 3, 5, 7, and 9. There is a guide to what needs to be discussed in those meetings, but there is time for open discussions (that lead to outcomes!) during the hour. The following is the process for the HOLAs; the process for Progress Leaders is very similar.

Week	HOLA/SLT line manager
1	Analysis of individuals, groups and classes using RAISE, SISRA, progress reports and transition matrices. Review updated SEF. Complete quarterly action plan. Shared agenda items.
3	Separate KS3 and KS4 meeting for Progress Leaders and subject leads to share approaches being taken for this quarter.
5	Mid-cycle review of Q action plan. Shared agenda items.
7	Mid-cycle review of Q action plan. Shared agenda items.
9	SEF update. Shared agenda items.

Prior to the start of the academic year, the HOLA will have already completed the following documents:

- Learning Area SEF
- Learning Area improvement plan
- Review of Year 11 and 13 results
- Examiner's Reports & eQLA
- Review of last year's Q4 data

Armed with this information the HOLA will draw up an action plan for the quarter. The three key issues from the updated SEF will be listed, and for each there will be:

- Group of students to be impacted
- Actions
- Success criteria

Q1 Action plan

WIG 80% 5A-C inc E&M, 0.8 Progress 8

Issue from SEF		
Group of students to be impacted	**Actions**	**Success criteria**
Issue from SEF		
Group of students to be impacted	**Actions**	**Success criteria**
Issue from SEF		
Group of students to be impacted	**Actions**	**Success criteria**

Even though there will likely be in excess of three issues, we believe that focusing on more than this would not be possible. This is an extension of the WIG principles. The action plan (and its review) forms the starting point of subsequent conversations. The end of the cycle brings an updating of the SEF, and the whole process repeats itself again. This is summarised in the chart below.

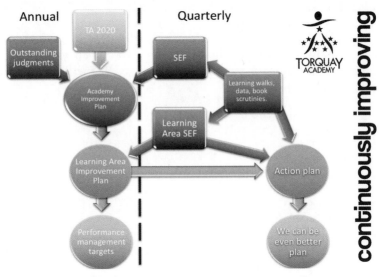

A nine-week cycle of curriculum improvement

HOLAs lead a weekly meeting with the teachers in their learning area. The meetings follow the nine-week teaching and learning cycles. There is a set agenda for each of the weekly meetings:

1. A review is undertaken of the previous cycle's teaching materials. What worked and what didn't work? What could be done differently next year? Changes to planning and resources are made while things are still fresh in the mind.

2. The data sheets from the previous cycle will have been printed in readiness for this meeting so teachers can update their T&L packs. The rest of the meeting continues with the previous week's work.

3. TLAC training to focus on a technique that supports the current needs of the learning area.

4. Write and review materials for the following cycle. Green stickers, assessments and knowledge organisers are completed. They are then handed in for checking.

5. Teachers jointly plan the next cycle's materials. Different learning areas divide up their team to meet their needs. This has resulted in some teams having specialist Key Stage materials preparation teams. There is a focus on embedding TLAC strategies into the resources.

6. Continue with the next cycle's joint planning.

7. Action plan developed in response to learning walk outcomes.

8. HOLA priority. This flexibility enables the team to spend additional time on what needs doing.

9. Teacher reflection meetings to analyse data and plan superteaching week.

A nine-week cycle of monitoring

HOLAs are responsible for the quality of teaching in their learning areas. Every quarter during weeks 5 and 6 they, along with their SLT line manager, will undertake learning walks. For every lesson they visit they will record www (what went well) and ebi (even better if) under the following headings:

- Routines – Expectations/TLAC/typicality
- Do Now – Engaging/immediate
- Success Criteria – Purpose of the lesson is clear/understanding what they are doing will impact on future assessments
- Engagement/BFL – No wasted time/student behaviours do not affect learning
- Books – Quality/volume/marking
- T&L Pack – Complete/fit for purpose
- Literacy – Evidence from different sources
- Pace/challenge/progress – Is progress visible or do students seem to be making progress over time?
- SLANT/silence is silence – Student body language/listening
- Displays – Relevant/condition

Feedback is given to teachers after the learning walks. The teachers can share any ebi with their coach to improve them. They are also able to use this feedback as part of their performance management if they choose to do so.

The HOLA will then produce a summary sheet using the headings above for their learning area. During the HOLA's meeting in week 7, this summary is discussed, and the learning area teachers come up with an action plan to develop the www and incorporate the ebi.

There is also a regular programme of book scrutinies. Each quarter every learning area submit a batch of named students' books to SLT to look at in the morning. The batch may change each quarter and is based upon the whole-school priority at the time – for example, the most able or disadvantaged. This allows us to track students across subjects and ensure all groups' books are meeting our high expectations. The HOLA comes to SLT briefing, and the quality of the books is discussed. Again, www and ebi are identified and fed back to the team using the following categories:

- Frequency/up to date
- Appropriate formative comments
- Students response – purple
- Marking for literacy
- Neatness/volume

Twice a year, during week 6 of quarters 1 and 3, we undertake a whole-school book scrutiny. HOLAs, TLR holders and their SLT link will look at books in every class in every year group for every teacher. This deep dive gives a detailed picture of the quality of student work. Records are kept under the same headings as above and discussed during the week 7 meeting; the focus is on sharing best practice and eliminating poor practice.

Similarly, the Progress Leaders are expected to monitor the quality of the tutors in their team. They also undertake a learning walk during week 6 using the following headings:

- Line up – Silence, tutors 'be seen looking' and small talk, silent walk in with assigned routes & door holders.
- Equipment check – Speed and reporting.
- Register – Use of 'good morning'.
- Activity – Page in book for reading/volume of work done.
- Dismissal – Orderly and routines. Threshold.
- Assembly – Silent entry and routine of where to sit.

Again, feedback is given to the tutors after the learning walks, and the Progress Leader produces a summary sheet. The team will discuss this during their next briefing and seek to make improvements.

KEY POINT

However you monitor your school it is vital that you have a full understanding of what is happening in every classroom.

Finances

Many decisions have a financial implication. Our Principal Finance Director, Claire Beckett, maintains an up-to-date three-year financial plan. This ensures that any ideas can be costed and then the impact of any additional spend can be seen for the next three years.

Key action points

- ☐ Are you happy with the carving-up of responsibilities within SLT?
- ☐ Do the SLT meetings meet your needs? If not, change them.
- ☐ Could the middle leaders contribute more on whole-school issues?
- ☐ A three-year plan can give a greater sense of direction than a one-year plan.
- ☐ What are your WIGs? Share them with everyone.
- ☐ How honest is your SEF?
- ☐ How can you ensure your school improvement isn't just held in an out-of-date improvement plan?
- ☐ How effective are line-management meetings?

Ideas you can implement in your school

- ☐ A quick catch up with the senior team can save numerous emails and keep you all on the same page.
- ☐ Place key items on SLT agendas as standing items.
- ☐ Use Varma's tool to decide which areas of school improvement to focus on.
- ☐ How do you share your three-year plan with the school community? A local signwriter could place it on a wall.
- ☐ Record outcomes, not minutes. It will save time and keep the focus on what needs to be done.
- ☐ Holding 121s will give you quality time to focus on school improvement.
- ☐ Can you find time in the school calendar to allow teachers to jointly plan?

Acknowledgments

Torquay Academy's improvement journey hasn't been based on a set of ideas that I, or the leaders within the school, have thought up and implemented. Almost all these ideas have come as a result of other school leaders and teachers being exceptionally generous with their time and welcoming us into their schools or by writing about their experiences. I have never met many of those who have had such a profound impact on my leadership and those around me. We are indebted to all of those who have supported, either directly or indirectly, our journey. I would particularly like to thank Kieran Earley, Roy Pike, Andy Buck, Doug Lemov, Neville Coles, Graeme Browne, Peter Matthews, Sir David Carter, Chris Penford, Carole Church, Jonathan Gower, and Ann Berger.

This book is not the definitive way of running a school; it is simply one way. It is our way. I hope that this book contributes to the pool of knowledge that exists and that somebody else may benefit from our experience. If you have ideas that you think we are missing, please do get in touch to let us know.

I am privileged to work with the most amazing group of teachers and support staff. Their dedication and commitment know no bounds. They have a relentless determination to ensure everyone succeeds. Thank you.

Biography and context

Steve joined Torquay Academy in 2014. It is a mixed 11–18 school based in a coastal town; it opened its sixth form in 2013. Within its small local authority there are three grammar schools, one with a grammar stream, one faith school and three community schools. Its catchment area varies greatly in its demographics and includes wards that are among the most deprived in England. 40% of its pupils are classified as disadvantaged and 92% are White British. Five GCSE passes including maths and English stood at 28% in 2014; this figure had increased to 74% by 2017. It is now heavily oversubscribed.